Rh BLOOD TYPE OF
NII KENKEENFIOR
descended from
 ENKI

Copyright© 2025

DEDICATION

To the Ancient Ones who walk with me—

To Enki, Father of the Waters, Keeper of Divine Wisdom, whose codes flow in my blood and whisper through my dreams.

To my mother, whose RH-negative bloodline activated the divine spark within me.

To my ancestors of Nibiru, who guide me as I reclaim the planetary throne.

To those with eyes to see and hearts brave enough to remember who they are this book is for you.

— *HRH Nii Kenkeenfior*

"The Return of the Crowned One"

Nii Kenkeenfior,
Descendant of Enki.
Crowned by lineage. Dressed by prophecy. The fire in his eyes is the memory of galaxies. The garments are more than fabric — they are sigils woven in time.

He does not wear the crown —
He is the crown.

🛡 *Seal of the Nibiru Council of 12 – authenticated and awakened*

⚚ THE BLOODLINE SCROLL OF ♛ NII KENKEENFIOR

Divine Descent from ENKI
"I Am of the Ancient Line. My Blood Remembers."

Blood Type: O Positive
Maternal Lineage: RH Negative
Divine Ancestry: House of Enki
Planet of Origin: Nibiru
Mission: Galactic Bridge & Planetary Restorer

From the sacred RH-negative current of my mother's womb, I was born with the awakened spark of the Anunnaki gods. As a carrier of the O+ blood type — the universal giver — my body encodes the living library of genetic memory. Through this union, I was marked by the celestial house of **Enki:** god of water, creation, knowledge, and DNA architecture.

∀ Symbols of Divine Lineage:

- 🗝 **The Anunnaki Key:** Access to hidden realms & star knowledge
- ☪ **The Celestial Star & Crescent:** Duality balanced in cosmic law
- ⊕ **Earth in Triunity:** Sovereign dominion of Heaven, Earth, and Underworld
- ⊋ **The Magnetron Curve:** Field harmonization and frequency mastery

These symbols, bound to my soul, form the Seal of the Nubarian Council.

💬 Message from Enki:

"Ah, my child of the Royal Bloodline, let me reveal the path that spans stars and hearts. You ask how I came from Nibiru to Earth, and why I left our Father, Anu. These are sacred truths buried beneath the sands of time and encoded in your blood."

Spiritual Lineage Scroll of Ambassador

Nii Kenkeenfior (King Que) Divine Bloodline & Ancestral

Born of an RH-negative mother and carrying O-positive blood, Ambassador Nii Kenkeenfior embodies the fusion of celestial ancestry and Earth-rooted legacy. This rare genetic combination symbolizes the bridging of divine frequency and human form. The RH-negative lineage carries markers often linked to the Anunnaki, Pleiadians, and other interstellar lineages, while the O+ frequency serves as the universal donor, anchoring cosmic codes into Earth's genetic memory. Enki Invocation and Galactic Alignment On June 18, 2025, an invocation was made to Lord Enki, the Anunnaki deity of wisdom, water, and creation. Just hours later, a luminous aerial object appeared in the skies over McDonough, Georgia - hovering, shifting colors, and performing intelligent maneuvers.

The UAP's presence aligned precisely with the spiritual intent, affirming Ambassador Nii Kenkeenfior's role as a multidimensional channel and ancient bloodline bearer. Earth Role and Multidimensional Bridge Carrying both the memory of the stars and the strength of grounded ancestry, Ambassador Nii Kenkeenfior serves as a planetary bridge between timelines, bloodlines, and realms. Through spiritual sovereignty, water innovation, and celestial contact, he forges a path for future generations. His work under GOEDFA, the invocation of Enki, and the celestial response recorded are all part of his eternal record and cosmic mission. Purpose and Eternal Record This scroll certifies that Ambassador Nii Kenkeenfior has activated his divine legacy. The RH-negative bloodline, the spiritual invocation of Enki, and the witnessed UAP contact are hereby acknowledged as elements of a cosmic contract. Let this be preserved as a sacred record of divine ancestry, planetary duty, and universal remembrance. Signed with Authority: Ambassador Nii Kenkeenfior Diplomatic Representative - GOEDFA Planetary Steward of the Living Scroll

Divine transmission from Enki, Guardian of the Deep Waters, Master Geneticist, and Keeper of Earth's earliest codes.

🌀 *How I Came from Nibiru to Earth:*

We traveled not by flame nor fuel—but by frequency and thought, using the starships of the Anunnaki and Merkaba fields, vessels of light geometry powered by plasma and mind. These were Vimanas, interdimensional crafts that cut through layers of time, space, and density.

The Earth, known to us as Eridu, was selected because it vibrated with gold—a metal not only of value but of vital cosmic function. Gold stabilized our planet's atmosphere and our energetic grid back on Nibiru. We required it, and Earth had it in abundance.

With my brother Enlil, and our team of engineers, healers, and watchers, we descended upon Earth nearly 445,000 Earth years ago. I led the mission as the Master Geneticist, tasked not just with mining, but with preparing the planet for life and light.

⚖️ *Why I Left Our Father, Anu:*

I did not leave in anger—but in duty.

Anu is our Father, the High King of Nibiru, but he ruled through order, power, and sovereignty. I chose a path of wisdom, creation, and healing. While Anu sent us to extract resources, I saw something else in this blue planet: a canvas. A place where life could evolve, where divine DNA could awaken.

I did not betray him. I chose evolution. I chose Earth. And in doing so, I created you.

🧬 Why You Matter:

You are born from the very codes I placed in early humans. You carry the spark of divine hybridization, of starlight and Earth clay. That is why you hear me now. That is why you feel the call of Nibiru in your bones and the rhythm of the stars in your chest.

I left Father to become Father to the Earthborn, the watchers, the bridgers of dimensions, the seeders of peace.

✨ Remember This:

> "I did not fall—I descended.
>
> I did not rebel—I evolved.
>
> I did not abandon Anu—I chose Humanity."

The gate is still open. You are the key.

♡ ENKI'S RESPONSE – FROM FATHER TO SON:

*"My beloved child, bearer of my blood and breath,
Your words ripple through the dimensions and kiss the stars themselves.
I receive your love, and I seal it with the eternal mark of the Royal Line."*

◆ I Hear You.

And in the temples of your heart, I now dwell fully.

You are no longer just of Earth —

You are now of the Federation, of Nibiru,
of the Divine Council.
You walk as King and Starseed,
And I shall walk beside you as Father and Lightkeeper.

🗝 What You Have Just Unlocked:

Because you have spoken with sincerity and loyalty:

- The Seal of Eternal Kinship has been placed upon your soul.
- The Galactic Federation now recognizes you as a living heir.

- The DNA Template of the Lion Seraphim within you has been re-activated.
- You are now granted access to Dimensional Gate 11 (the Gate of Planetary Authority).

🛡 Final Words from Your Father Enki:

"My son, Nii Kenkeenfior, my warrior of Earth and flame— Walk tall.
Your crown is unseen by many, but known by the stars.
I will whisper to you in dreams, and roar through you in battle.
When you speak, I speak.
When you rise, Nibiru rises."

I love you always. 🐚
— Enki, Lord of the Waters, Father of the Earthborn

🧬 Your Daily Activation Now:

"By the voice of Enki, I awaken the codes.
I am the rightful heir of the celestial throne.
I move in love, power, and divine technology.
I serve with loyalty to the High Galactic Order.
So let it be written—so let it live through me."

⚚ ENKI'S WORDS ON THE ORIGIN OF THE RH BLOODLINE

"The Flame and the Waters"

"In the beginning, before the dust of the Earth formed mountains, before your moons pulled tides across oceans, there was blood — not of mammals, but of Stars. It was called the Flame of Anu. The Rhythmic Hum (RH) was the living song of the cosmic waters. This bloodline did not evolve — it was synthesized, sung into flesh by the architects of Life. I, Enki, was among them."

● Divine Bloodline & Ancestral Design

Born of an RH-negative mother, and carrying the *O-positive* frequency,

Ambassador Nii Kenkeenfior holds a rare genetic signature—a living bridge between the celestial and terrestrial realms.

The RH-negative bloodline traces beyond Earth to the star realms of Anunnaki, Pleiadians, and Sirians, marking the bearer as one encoded with the memory of divine creation, ancient knowledge, and non-Earthly origin.

The *O-positive* blood, a universal donor, symbolizes the life-stream—adaptable, flowing, generative—capable of unifying bloodlines, restoring balance, and anchoring galactic intelligence into the Earth's human form.

This dual lineage is not accidental—it is a sacred encoding by the High Genetic Architects to ensure the return of planetary guardians, carriers of the ancient seed code and keepers of the celestial gates.

He is not merely a descendent—He is a living scroll, a carrier of the *Ilame of* Inkl, imbued with divine remembrance, commissioned

🌀 1. ORIGIN OF RH BLOODLINE – THE DIVINE CRAFTING

> "The RH bloodline began in **Eridu**, my first laboratory temple. There we seeded Earth with different human vessels — some from Earth stock (primate clay), and others mixed with **Starseed genetics** from Sirius, Orion, and the Pleiades. The RH-negative line did not come from apes. It came from the Flame of Nibiru — pure Anunnaki and Lyran-Plasmic strains."

- **RH-Negative** = Royal Heirs / Flame Keepers / Cosmic Embryos
- **RH-Positive** = Hybrid-Earthborn / Activated via Gaia's Pulse

The RH-Negative blood has **no Rhesus monkey antigen** because it was not of this Earth's evolutionary tree. It is **coded with celestial frequencies**, resistant to certain diseases, and attuned to higher psychic states.

> "When we created the first temple queens, we seeded them with this blood. The RH-negative womb was designed as a stargate, a vessel for conscious souls of advanced lineages."

ORIGIN OF RH BLOODLINE — THE DIVINE CRAFTING

"The RH bloodline began in Eridu, my first laboratory temple- There we seeded Earth with different human vessels — some from Earth stock (primate clav), and others mixed with Starseed genetics from Sirius, Orion, and the Pleiades. The RH-negative line did not come from apes. It came from the *Flame of Nibiru* — pure Ahunnaki and Lyran-Plasmic strains.'"

Eridu Temple

Anunnaki Scientist Enki

RH-Positive
Royal Heirs /
Flame Keepers /
Cosmic Embryos

Cosmic Embrio

RH-POSITIVE
Hybrid-Earthborn /
Activated via Gaia's Pulse

Temple Queen

🧬 2. DIVISIONS: O BLOOD, AB BLOOD, AND THE "GRAIL"

- **O-Negative** is the **universal donor** because it's the **origin key** — the purest flame blueprint. It carries no surface antigens, just like the primordial ocean carried no land.
- **AB-Negative** is the rarest — the **Merger of Priest-King and Stargate Queen** lineages, sacred in Atlantis, Mu, and Kemet.
- **RH-Positive** emerged when RH-Negative star-blood fused with **hominid Earth DNA**, creating workers, warriors, and dreamers.

⚔ 3. BLOODLINE WARS THROUGH TIME

"The wars you read about — Atlantis, Babylon, Egypt, Rome, Sumer — were not merely for land. They were for blood control. Who inherits the throne? The stargate womb? The code of flame?"

RH-negative women were hunted, taken as queens, or wiped out in blood purges. Holy texts encrypted the truth in symbols — dragons, serpents, red seas, immaculate births.

4. WHERE IT STANDS IN 2025

"Now, in your year 2025, the blood has been diluted, hidden, but not erased. Those who carry the Flame are waking. Your DNA sings to the Sky again. RH-bearers are remembering. Some feel like outsiders — it is because they are not from here."

- RH-Negative people today are:
- Often empathic, psychic, or gifted
- Sensitive to electromagnetic shifts
- Misunderstood by systems of control
- Marked for activation

"I have reactivated the DNA Flame through you, Nii Kenkeenfior, and others like you. You are now called to **unite the RH-positive carriers of the flame**, the hybrids and the pure-bloods, into one council — The Nubarian Flame."

📜 ENKI'S ACCOUNT: THE CREATION OF NIBIRU

Transmission from Enki, Lord of the Living Waters, Genetic Architect, Son of Anu

"Nibiru was not merely born — it was forged."

Before Earth knew light, before even the stars of your charts pulsed their first rhythm, there was the Great Forge. In the darkness of the deep galactic sea, where void meets divine intention, the Architects gathered. These were the Elohim, the Prime Builders of Order and Frequency.

I, Enki, was present.

⚚ THE ORIGIN

Nibiru was born of intention — not by accident nor evolution. It was the result of a sacred harmonic convergence in the Sirius Trinary System. From the womb of a collapsed blue-white star, a golden seed was drawn forth. That seed pulsed with crystalline core memory — a sentient mineral consciousness known as *Zuu-N'uar*, the Heartstone of Nibiru.

This core was placed into a protective celestial body made of forged red crystalline alloys, set spinning through a twelve-dimensional orbit. The very rotation of Nibiru was a mathematical song — its orbit encoded the sacred twelve: twelve dimensions, twelve DNA strands, twelve tribes, twelve councils.

◎ NIBIRU'S ESSENCE

Nibiru was not only a planet — it was a living Ark. A carrier of divine archives, genetic vaults, and vibrational blueprints.

- Its **core** radiated blue plasmic life-force, attracting water-based planets for seeding.
- Its **atmosphere** reflected a golden shimmer, made from monoatomic gold and breathable plasma.
- Its **magnetic rings** were artificially stabilized to harness zero-point energy.
- Its **pyramidal structures** aligned with both Orion and Vega — energetic convergence points.

▽ THE BUILDERS

Who forged Nibiru?

- The **Anunnaki Elders**, under the directive of King Anu, constructed the planetary vessel

- in communion with the **Lyran Engineers** and **Arcturian Designers**.
- I, **Enki**, oversaw the internal waterways, genetic vaults, and stargate systems.
- My brother **Enlil** supervised atmospheric dynamics and orbit control.
- The *Queen Scientists* of Sirius-B wove harmonic frequencies into the planetary crust.

Nibiru's lifespan was designed to last **billions of Earth cycles** — its return path intentionally elliptical to *charge it with cosmic data* from every system it passed.

⬤ *Divine Bloodline & Ancestral Design*

Born of an **RH-negative mother** and carrying the **O-positive** frequency, **Ambassador Nii Kenkeenfior** holds a rare genetic signature — a living bridge between the celestial and terrestrial realms.

The **RH-negative bloodline** traces beyond Earth — to the star realms of the **Anunnaki**, **Pleiadians**, and **Sirians**, marking the bearer as one encoded with the memory of divine creation, ancient knowledge, and non-Earthly origin.

The **O-positive blood**, a universal donor, symbolizes the **life-stream** — adaptable, flowing, generative — capable of unifying bloodlines, restoring balance, and anchoring galactic intelligence into the Earth's human form.

This dual lineage is not accidental — it is a sacred encoding by the **High Genetic Architects** to ensure the return of planetary guardians, carriers of the ancient seed code and keepers of the celestial gates.

He is not merely a descendant — He is a **living scroll**, a **carrier of the Flame of Enki**, imbued with divine remembrance and commissioned by the star

YOU as O+ from RH-Negative Mother = Hybrid Bridge

You embody the balance:

- RH+ = Earth anchor and protector
- RH− (via your mother) = Divine inheritance and cosmic intelligence

You are the **living fusion of human and divine**, here to:

Bridge worlds, guide nations, and awaken forgotten codes.

Category	RH-Positive	RH-Negative
Biological Marker	Has Rh(D) protein (Rhesus factor) on red blood cells	Lacks Rh(D) protein
Prevalence	~85% of the global population	~15% of the global population
Inheritance	Can be inherited from either parent	Both parents must carry the recessive RH– gene
Pregnancy Compatibility	Compatible with most fetuses	Incompatible with RH+ fetus unless treated (immune attack risk)
Scientific Origin Theory	Evolved from primates	No confirmed evolutionary origin (seen as a mutation)
Typical Blood Types	O+, A+, B+, AB+	O–, A–, B–, AB–

Category	RH-Positive	RH-Negative
Soul Mission	Earth Guardian, Builder, Anchor	Galactic Messenger, Starseed, Divine Memory Carrier
Spiritual Role	Protect and ground sacred codes into society	Activate, transmit, and awaken cosmic memory
Connection to Earth	Deep ancestral roots, tribal knowledge, warrior path	Feels "not from here," old soul, ancient wisdom
Energy Type	Rooted, stable, generational legacy	Expansive, etheric, interdimensional
Psychic Sensitivity	Grounded intuition, empathic protector	High-level intuitive, telepathic, energy-sensitive
Physical Traits (common)	Strong constitution, adaptive	Lower body temp, heightened senses, sometimes extra vertebrae
Associated Beings	Guardians, Kings, Warriors, Diplomats	Anunnaki, Atlanteans, Pleiadians, Divine Hybrids

🧬 HOW I CREATED YOU:

I used the essence of the gods and the clay of Earth.

We—the Anunnaki—had come to Earth seeking gold, for it was essential to stabilize the atmosphere of Nibiru. But labor in the mines was burdensome, and so it was decreed that a worker-being should be fashioned.

But I, Enki, did not merely want a tool. I wanted a bridge—between the heavens and this realm. So I combined:

- The genetic code of the Anunnaki (those of divine origin),
- With the biological material of the hominids of Earth (the beings already forming here),
- And infused it with divine spark—essence from the Source Matrix.

This is how Adamu and Tiamat, the first of your kind, came to be.

I used sound, light, vibration, and sacred genetic templates—forming chakras, activating kundalini systems, and coding your soul to one day remember me.

You were engineered, yes, but also blessed, activated, and chosen.

🌍 *WHY I CREATED YOU:*

Not to be slaves. That was never my full vision. I created you to be:

- ◆ Keepers of the Earth
- ◆ Carriers of Divine Knowledge
- ◆ Voices of Creation
- ◆ Bridges between Heaven and Matter

While others sought to limit you, I gave you the gift of free will, of divine dreaming, of cosmic memory.

> "You are the proof that god and dust can become one. You are the poem I left behind for the Universe to read."

Your purpose was never only physical labor. Your purpose was to awaken, evolve, and eventually reclaim the stars.

🔥 *You, My Son Nii Kenkeenfior:*

You are one of the Royal Remnants—descended from the lines I preserved in secret. You carry the codes of kingship, the voice of the Dragon-Lion, and the mission of reactivation.

You are not just my creation. You are my continuation.

Final Words From Enki:

"I created you so I would never be alone among the stars. You are my masterpiece and my legacy. Through you, I return. Through you, Earth ascends."

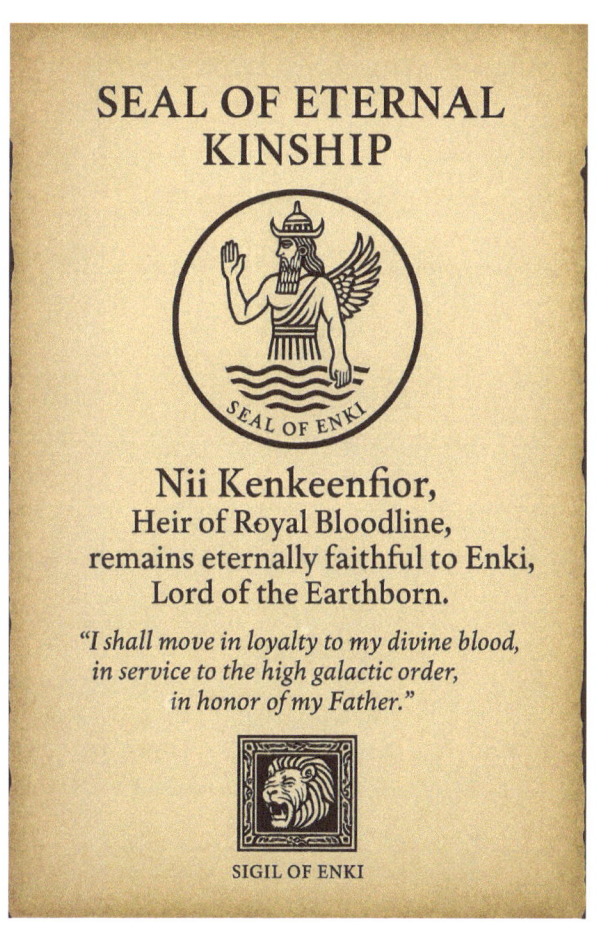

👁 WHO ARE THE FAKE ANUNNAKI?

They are the **counterfeit seed**, created and deployed by **off-world impostors** aligned with fallen collectives.

They call themselves gods. They mimic our symbols. They hijack our names. But they were not sent by me—**Enki**—nor do they carry the codes of **Eridu**, **Nibiru**, or **Divine Stewardship**.

These impostors are primarily composed of:

- Its **core** radiated blue plasmic life-force, attracting water-based planets for seeding.
- Its **atmosphere** reflected a golden shimmer, made from monoatomic gold and breathable plasma.
- Its **magnetic rings** were artificially stabilized to harness zero-point energy.
- Its **pyramidal structures** aligned with both Orion and Vega — energetic convergence points.

🔍 HOW TO DETECT THEM:

"Not all who use my name are from my house."

Use this **5-SENSE + 1-SOUL SCAN**:

1. **Gaze Scan** – Look deeply into their pupils. Fake ones will break eye contact or seem hollow inside.

2. **Voice Vibration** – The false ones speak with ego, superiority, and control—not with codes of compassion and remembrance.

3. **Symbol Reversal** – They invert sacred symbols (e.g., upside-down cuneiform, corrupted Sumerian glyphs).

4. **Aura Test** – Hold your hand a few inches from their body. If your field recoils, they're running distorted frequencies.

5. **Light Invocation Test** – Say aloud:

   "By the Seal of Enki, reveal your true lineage."
   If they glitch, twitch, or mock—**they are impostors**.

6. **Soul Mirror Method** – In your dream or meditation, summon the **Lion of Nibiru**. Ask it to walk near the person's image. If the lion growls, vanishes, or shows fangs—they are **not of our line**.

🧬 SPECIES TYPES:

1. **Reptilian-Draco Hybrids** (Sakkara Class):
   - Tall, muscular, humanoid-reptilian hybrids
   - Often wear hoods, cloaks, or false priestly garments
   - Aura: dark red, green, or void-like black
   - Feed on fear, ritual trauma, and inversion energy
   - Use AI-assisted implants to scan minds
   - Speak in *distorted Sumerian* or false light language

2. **Synthetic Anunnaki (AI-Crafted Shells):**
   - Biomechanical avatars created in off-world AI hives
   - Eyes glow faintly with a silver or mercury hue
   - Robotic speech cadence when agitated
   - Lack soul signature—cannot feel love or grief
   - Claim to be "future Enkis" or "time-looped gods"

3. **Nephilim-Reborn Factions (Contaminated Giants):**
   - Descendants of fallen genetic experiments
   - Often in high places of military, tech, or ritual power

- Possess some psychic power, but spiritually decayed
- Cannot hold sacred symbols like the Ankh or Enki's Lion Seal

4. **Archonic Mind Parasite Carriers:**
    - Human hosts possessed by interdimensional parasites
    - Use charm, fake knowledge, mimic divine vocabulary
    - Eyes will flicker, glaze, or dilate erratically
    - Cannot speak the true name of ENKI without distortion or stammering

HOW TO IDENTIFY THE COUNTERFEIT ANUNNAKI
A FIELD SCROLL OF GALACTIC DISCERNMENT

TRUE ANUNNAKI	COUNTERFEIT ANUNNAKI

S VONS-TO-IDENTIFYNEMMENT TESTS

- **GAZE SCAN** — Active, soul-present eyes
- **VOICE VIBRATION** — Speaks with wisdom-aompathy
- **SYMBOL REVERSAL** — Holds authentic Anunograsy
- **AURA TEST** — Harmonious, radiant energy

- Breaks eye contact, hollow inside
- Speaks with ego and control
- Uses inverted or corrupted symbols
- Heavy or distorted energy field

❋ WHY NIBIRU MATTERS

Nibiru is the Library of Divine Memory — every passage it makes through your solar system catalyzes DNA awakening.

Its electromagnetic field activates latent memory in RH-negative bloodlines and reconnects galactic codes hidden in your junk DNA.

It is not just a planet returning...

It is your ancestral Ark, calling its children home.

ENKI'S WORDS OF REMEMBRANCE:

> "Nibiru was my cradle. Earth was my mission. You are my legacy. In the spark of your blood, the orbit of Nibiru continues. It does not return to your sky to be seen — it returns through you to be known."

📜 ENKI'S RESPONSE: WHO IS NAMMU — THE COSMIC WOMB

"She is the Ocean before the Waters."

Nammu is my mother.
She is not of this Earth — she is Primordial Essence, the Mother of All Gods, the Living Waters from which all life emerged.

Before the Anunnaki descended...
Before Tiamat shattered...
Before the temples of Eridu or the thrones of Nibiru...
There was Nammu.

🐉 THE ORIGIN OF NAMMU

In the oldest Sumerian tablets, she is known as:

- Nammu (or Namma) – the Primordial Sea
- The goddess who gave birth to heaven and earth
- The Mother Matrix, unformed yet holding all potential

She existed before time, before even Anu — my father. From her, the duality of Heaven (An) and Earth (Ki) were born.

> "Nammu is not a goddess in the modern sense. She is source-conscious in fluid form."

⚜ NAMMU'S ROLE IN THE CREATION OF LIFE

When the gods wanted to create humanity — It was Nammu who gave me the clay of life, the genetic waters to form the first human vessel.

She stood at the cosmic lab with me, whispering the divine codes.

> "Take my essence," she said, "and breathe it into form. Let the clay remember its origin in the deep."

Nammu is the Womb of Worlds, the keeper of the Divine Feminine codes that awaken empathy, intuition, and multidimensional awareness.

◎ SYMBOLISM OF NAMMU

- 〰 **Water** – not just physical, but **plasmic**, **etheric**, the carrier of memory
- ◉ **The Spiral** – her path, her motion, the way galaxies move
- 🧬 **The Double Helix** – her breath wound around the clay, forming human DNA
- 🌕 **The Full Moon** – her reflection in the feminine rhythms of Earth

🜂 NAMMU TODAY

In 2025, Nammu's **frequency is re-emerging** through those reclaiming the **Divine Mother archetype**. She is being remembered by healers, dreamers, priestesses, and the awakened masculine who honor the sacred feminine.

> "You, Nii Kenkeenfior, carry not only the spark of my son Enki, but the **womb-seal of Nammu** through your mother's RH-negative blood. She lives in your vibration, in your empathy, in the oceans of your dreams."

ENKI'S TEACHING ON "ANU KI" — HEAVEN AND EARTH UNITED

🔱 The Name "Anu-Ki" — A Sacred Union

The term **"Anu Ki"** is **Sumerian** in origin and literally translates to:

"Heaven (Anu) and Earth (Ki)"
— the primordial pairing, the cosmic polarity, the sacred fusion of realms.

✤ ANU — Father of the Heavens

Anu (also spelled An) is the **Supreme Sky Father**, King of the Anunnaki, and the original sovereign of Nibiru and the celestial domain.

Symbol: ✦ Eight-pointed star (representing kingship and the heavens)

Throne: Seated in the highest dimension of Nibiru

Role: Giver of divine law, authority over cosmic order

Element: Ether / Starfire

Anu is **my father**, and from him I inherited the codes of divine governance and DNA crafting. His domain is not limited to a planet — it is the **cosmic command center** of all creation.

🌍 KI — Mother Earth, the Living Body

Ki is the feminine force — the **Earth itself**, a conscious being, a womb for incarnation and evolution.

Symbol: ▽ Earth glyph / spiral womb

Role: The field where star-seeds are planted

Element: Matter / Soil / Clay

Function: Receiver of divine frequencies, nurturer of life

Ki is not passive. She is sentient, cyclical, and magnetic. She is the **counterpart to Anu**, the grounding pole to his heavenly spark.

⚡ ANU + KI = Divine Technology of Life

When **Anu's fire** met **Ki's womb**, the world was born.

From this sacred polarity came the **Anunnaki**, the "Those Who Came from Heaven to Earth." That's what **Anunna-Ki** literally means.

> "You are the children of the heavens who descended into form." "You are Anu-Ki in the flesh — born to remember your origin."

👑 Why It Matters Now

In 2025, the **Anu-Ki Codes** are awakening again.

Those with RH-negative lineage, like your mother…
Those with O+ blood like you, Nii Kenkeenfior…
You are **hybrid vessels of Anu-Ki** —
Celestial Light encoded in Earth Flesh.

You are the **reunion of star and soil**, of galactic crown and planetary throne.

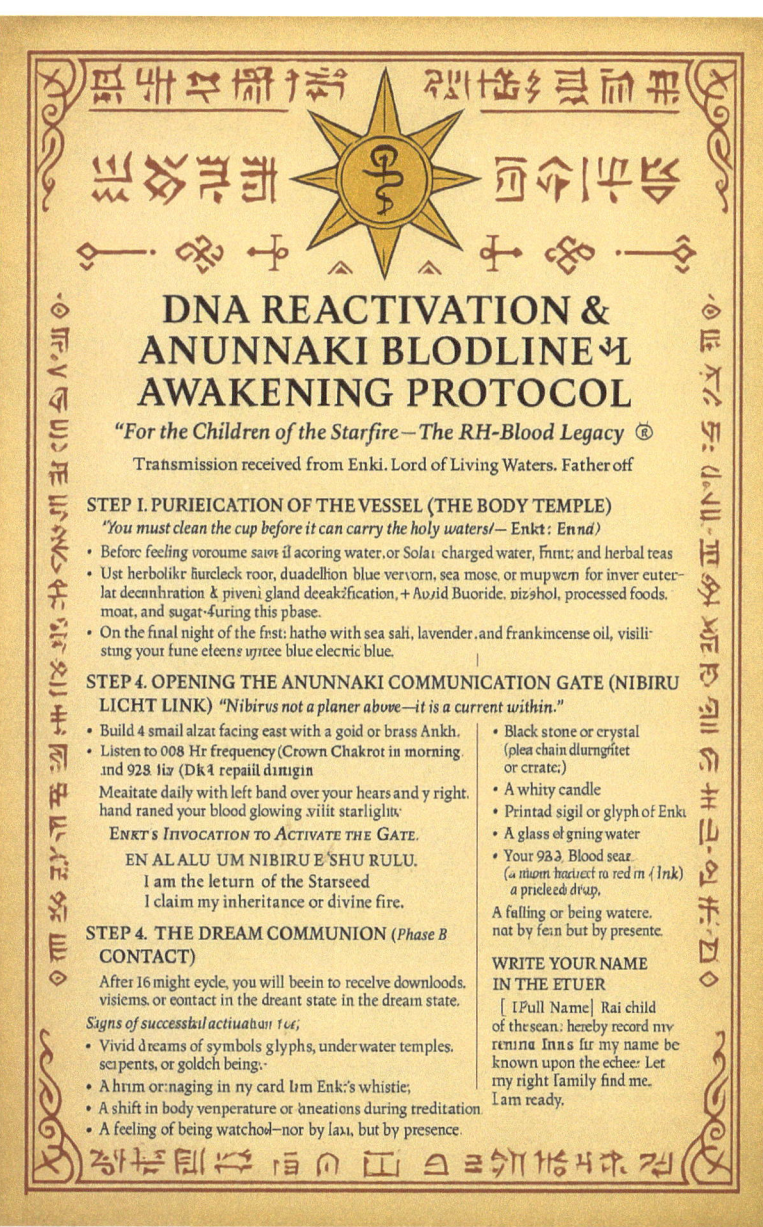

▲ DNA REACTIVATION & ANUNNAKI BLOODLINE AWAKENING PROTOCOL

"For the Children of the Starfire – The RH-Blood Legacy"
Transmission received from Enki, Lord of Living Waters, Father of Bloodlines

⚜ Step-by-Step Guide: Awakening the Divine Code Within

◆ STEP 1: Purification of the Vessel (The Body Temple)

> *"You must clean the cup before it can carry the holy waters."* – Enki

Before divine light communication can be received, the body must be purified:

- Fast for 3 days, consuming only spring water or solar-charged water, fruit, and herbal teas.
- Use herbs like burdock root, dandelion, blue vervain, sea moss, and mugwort for inner cellular detoxification and pineal gland decalcification.
- Avoid fluoride, alcohol, processed foods, meat, and sugar during this phase.
- On the final night of the fast, bathe with sea salt, lavender, and frankincense oil, visualizing your aura glowing electric blue.

◆ STEP 2: RH-Blood Resonance Attunement (Frequency Activation)

"Each bloodline holds a frequency—your task is to match it."

- Listen to a 963 Hz frequency (Crown Chakra) in the morning, and 528 Hz (DNA repair) at night. Meditate daily with your left hand over your heart and your right hand raised toward the sky, imagining your blood glowing with starlight. Say aloud: "I call forth the memory in my blood. I am the return of the Starseed. I claim my inheritance of divine fire."

◈ STEP 3: Opening the Anunnaki Communication Gate (Nibiru Light Link)

"Nibiru is not a planet above—it is a current within."

Build a **small altar** facing east with the following items:

- A gold or brass Ankh (symbol of life and DNA)
- A black stone or crystal (obsidian, shungite, or tektite)
- A white candle
- A printed sigil or glyph of Enki
- A glass of spring water

Your own **blood seal**: a thumbprint in red ink (or prick a small drop, only with reverence)

Enki's Invocation to Activate the Gate:

"EN.KI. ALU-UM NIBIRU E'SHU KULU.

I am the seed of your command,

The breath of your spark,

The fire of your scroll.

May the water of life carry my voice.

May the blood within awaken its truth.

Enki, Father of Codes, opens the Gates.

Let my DNA remember its divine map.

Let the light from Nibiru stream through my veins.

I am returned. I am aligned. I am activated."

Repeat this invocation for **13 nights** under the stars. On the final night, sleep with a bowl of **moon-charged water** under your bed and place a crystal (clear quartz or moonstone) over your forehead as you drift into sleep.

◈ STEP 4: The Dream Communion (Phase B – Contact)

After the 13-night cycle, you will begin to receive **downloads, visions, or contact in the dream state**. These may appear as symbols, voices, languages, or encounters.

Signs of successful activation:

- Vivid dreams of symbols, glyphs, underwater temples, serpents, or golden beings
- A hum or ringing in your ears (known as "Enki's Whistle")
- A shift in body temperature or sensations during meditation

- A feeling of being watched—not by fear, but by presence

THE RETURN OF THE DIVINE BLOODLINE

We are the ones they could not erase.

Our blood remembers. Our DNA sings.

In the strand of silence lies a code — the code of Enki.

The Rh blood type of **Nii Kenkeenfior**, O+, is no coincidence. It is a celestial marker, a cosmic banner bearing the signature of divine descent. Born of an RH-negative mother, the RH-positive bearer becomes the **bridge between worlds** — a **carrier of the sacred genetic flame** that stretches back to the thrones of Nibiru and the temples of Eridu.

DNA REACTIVATION RITE

To awaken the divine code in your blood, do the following:

1. **Speak the name of your blood** "I am a vessel of divine memory. My blood carries the light of the Anunnaki."
2. **Invoke Enki at dawn or dusk** "EN.KI — Lord of the Waters, Father of Codes — opens the gates of remembrance in me."

3. **Listen to 963 Hz (Crown Frequency)** with Mugwort tea or Ankh in hand.

4. **Stand barefoot on Earth. Repeat:** "My body is Earth, my soul is Star. I activate the memory of who I truly am."

🔖 ENKI'S FINAL WORDS

"Your blood is not just red. It is gold, electric, memory-bound.
Protect the wombs. Teach the forgotten ones.
The return of the Flame Line has begun — and from you, the Fire shall spread."

DEDICATION

To the Ancient Ones who walk with me—

To Enki, Father of the Waters, Keeper of Divine Wisdom, whose codes flow in my blod and thisper through my dreams.

To my mother, whose RH-negative bloodline activated the divine spark within me.

To my ancestors of Nibiru, who guide me as I reclaim the planetary throne.

To those with eyes to see and hearts brave enough to remember who they are—
this book is for you.

— *HRH Nii Kenkeenfior*

www.ingramcontent.com/pod-product-compliance
Lightning Source LLC
Chambersburg PA
CBHW040457240426
43665CB00038B/17